NATURE IN THE NEWS

THE TEXAS WILDFIRES

Therese Shea

PowerKiDS press™

New York

Published in 2007 by The Rosen Publishing Group, Inc.
29 East 21st Street, New York, NY 10010

Book Design: Dan Hosek, Michael Ruberto

Photo Credits: Cover (light effect) © Taewoon Lee/Shutterstock; cover (fire) © Peter Weber/ Shutterstock; interior background © Maja Schon/Shutterstock; p. 5 © Sascha Burkard/Shutterstock p. 7 © Dennis Rozie/Shutterstock; p. 9 © Shawn Talbot/Shutterstock; pp. 11, 17 © AFP/ Getty Images; p. 13 © Andrei Volkovets/Shutterstock; pp.15, 19, 21 © Getty Images; p. 23 © Dale A. Stork/Shutterstock; p. 25 © Emil Pozar/Shutterstock; p. 27 © Anna Galejeva/Shutterstock.

Library of Congress Cataloging-in-Publication Data

Shea, Therese.
  The Texas wildfires / Therese Shea.
      p. cm. — (Nature in the news)
  Includes bibliographical references and index.
  ISBN-13: 978-1-4042-3540-X
  ISBN-10: 1-4042-3540-X
  1. Wildfires—Texas—Juvenile literature. I. Title. II. Series.
  SD421.32.T4S54 2007
  363.37'909764—dc22
                                    2006015703

Manufactured in the United States of America

CONTENTS

WHAT IS A WILDFIRE?

A wildfire is a fast-moving fire that spreads across a country area. Wildfires are a danger to anything and anyone in their paths. People may start wildfires on purpose by dropping a match. They may accidentally start them when they are careless with a campfire. Wildfires can start naturally with a lightning strike, too. Once they start, they can be very hard to put out.

In December 2005, some areas of the United States began to face more wildfires than they had ever seen. In this book, we'll learn how several months of wildfires burning out of control in Texas affected thousands of people.

Many warmer areas of the United States experience weather that causes wildfires. ▶

5

FIRE SCIENCE

Three elements are needed for a fire to burn: high **temperatures**, fuel, and oxygen. When these elements come together in the right conditions, a **chemical reaction** occurs. The reaction releases energy in the form of fire.

Did you know that fuel like wood is not really what we see burning in a fire? Wood begins to break down in high temperatures. What we see burning is the gas that the wood gives off as it breaks down. When the wood is broken down into ash and has no more gas to give off, the fire stops.

Lightning may start fires in the wilderness. About 8 million lightning bolts hit Earth each day!

▶

6

You may have seen someone start a campfire with a match and dry wood. A campfirelike situation can happen in nature, too. Fuel is anything **flammable**, such as dry leaves and tree limbs. Oxygen is always available in the air. All that is needed is a heat source to provide the high temperatures needed to **ignite** the fire.

Once the fire is ignited, it can cause great harm if it is not controlled. More fuel creates higher temperatures. Higher temperatures make the fire spread more quickly. If the fire spreads quickly, it finds even more fuel. A fire can "feed" itself in this way.

A crown fire is a wildfire that spreads through the tops of trees. Animals and people on the ground below may not be able to breathe because so much oxygen is sucked upward into the fire.

Rain, Drought, and the "Tinderbox"

You may be surprised to learn that rainfall contributed to the 2005–2006 Texas wildfires. Areas of Texas had received more rain than usual for a few years before the fires started. This caused plants, grass, bushes, and shrubs to grow in places where little **vegetation** had grown before. Then, low **humidity** and very high temperatures caused a **drought** late in 2005. The soil lost moisture and the new plants dried up. These dried-up plants became the perfect fuel for wildfires.

Some scientists think that La Niña caused the Texas winter drought. "La Niña" is a term that describes unusually cold temperatures in the eastern Pacific Ocean. It affects weather all over Earth.

The governor of Texas, Rick Perry, described his state as a "tinderbox." A tinderbox is a metal box that holds flammable **materials** that can be easily ignited. Governor Perry meant that parts of Texas were so dry that they were like fuel in a box, ready to go up in flames once someone lit a match.

We don't know how the first wildfires started in late December 2005. Some think the fires may have been started by people burning trash, setting off fireworks, or throwing away lit cigarettes. Whatever the source, strong winds spread the fires, which quickly became wildfires.

Campfires that are not properly tended may cause wildfires.

▶

FIRE IN CROSS PLAINS, TEXAS

Strong winds made the Texas wildfires very hard to **extinguish**. A campfire will burn out once the fire has used up all of its fuel. A wildfire spread by wind continuously finds more and more fuel to keep it burning. Although it may move quickly, this kind of wildfire is called a crawling fire because it "crawls" along the ground, burning through low vegetation.

How flammable can dry grass be? One man reported that air around a wildfire was so hot that grass started on fire 50 feet (15 m) from the flames! Wind, heat, and dry grass led one wildfire into the town of Cross Plains, Texas.

Texas governor Rick Perry asked the federal government to help Texans who lost their homes and businesses to wildfires. He also asked for more supplies and firefighters to fight the wildfires.

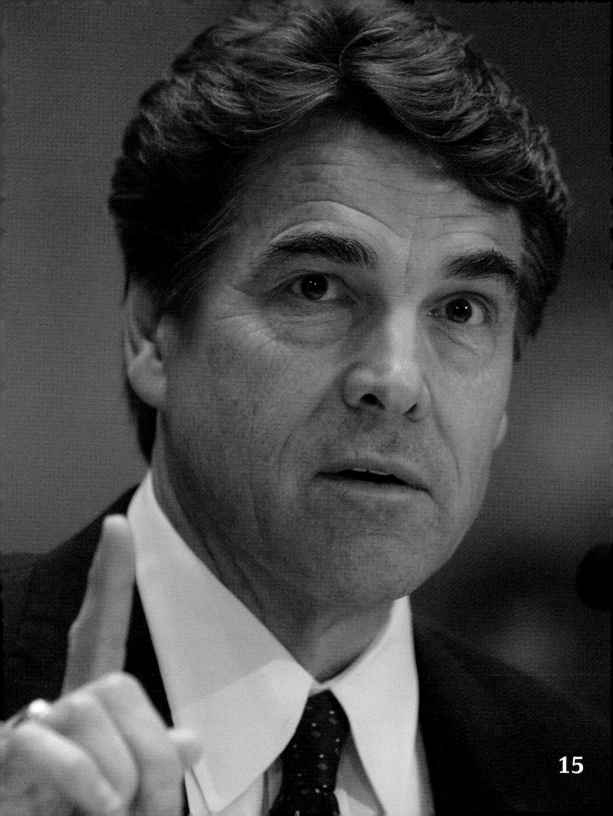

Cross Plains, Texas, is located about 150 miles (241 km) southwest of Dallas. It is a small town of about 1,000 people. On December 27, 2005, one townsperson was hanging clothes outside to dry. Suddenly, she saw a big ball of smoke in the distance. It was so big and moving so fast that at first she thought it was a **tornado**. She jumped into her car and left town immediately.

Firefighters from thirty-one departments arrived in Cross Plains to help battle the fire. Although they got the fire under control by midnight, two people had died and over 100 homes had been destroyed.

The wildfire's black smoke filled the air in Cross Plains, Texas. One firefighter said that the sky was as dark as midnight although it was the middle of the afternoon. ▶

FIGHTING WILDFIRE

How do firefighters fight wildfires like the one in Cross Plains? They try to remove one of the three elements needed for fire to burn: fuel, high temperatures, and oxygen.

Workers may first remove the fuel from the path of the fire. They clear the land of flammable materials, such as grass and wood. Then they may cover the burning land with water, which reduces the high temperature of the fire. They may also use chemicals, such as **fire retardants**, which block the oxygen in the air from reaching the fuel. Helicopters and planes are sometimes used to thoroughly cover a wildfire with water and fire retardant.

Firefighters called smokejumpers may be dropped by helicopter to fight fires in areas that are hard to reach by land.

Firefighters may dig a line around or in front of a fire, sometimes with a bulldozer. This is called a fireline or firebreak. The fireline keeps the fire from spreading and contains the fire in one area so firefighters can extinguish it more easily.

During the December 2005 and January 2006 Texas wildfires, the winds were often too strong to fly aircraft. Because the wildfires moved so fast, it was hard for firefighters to race to an area in front of the fire to stop it from spreading. Also, if the wind changed direction, the wildfire might travel to a different area from the one firefighters expected. One worker reported that the flames from a wildfire were moving faster than 30 miles (48 km) an hour!

These firefighters are creating a fireline. If winds are strong enough, a fire may "jump" across a fireline and light fuel on the other side.

"THE SINGLE WORST DAY"

The fires in Cross Plains, Texas, were extinguished. However, over the following 2 weeks, about 455,000 acres (184,275 h) of Texas land burned in more wildfires. Wildfires continued to break out over the next few months.

The Texas Forest Service called March 12, 2006, "the single worst day in Texas wildfire history." Many large wildfires broke out across the state. High winds made it risky for small aircraft to fly, grounding one of the best firefighting methods. Over a few days, about 691,000 acres (279,855 h) of land burned. Over 1,900 people had to **evacuate** their homes. Eleven people died from causes related to the fires.

Many people lost their homes and belongings during the wildfires that swept through Texas.

By April 2006, over 11,000 wildfires in Texas had burned almost 5 million acres (2 million h). Many areas did not have enough firefighters and equipment to fight the fires. Sometimes many fire departments were needed to put out a single fire. That meant fewer firefighters were available to put out fires in other places. Even an hour delay can allow wildfires to burn out of control.

In addition, many small towns had only volunteer firefighters and limited tools and money. After months of battling fires, Texas firefighters were exhausted from long hours of hard work. Gradually, fewer wildfires broke out as lower temperatures and heavy rain moved across the land.

Some states, such as Oklahoma and Arizona, loaned Texas firefighting air tankers. Texas aircraft dropped over 5.4 million gallons (20.4 million l) of fire retardant over 4 months.

▶

WILDFIRES IN OTHER STATES

The hot, dry weather that Texas had experienced during the winter of 2005–2006 also affected other southern states. Over 1,200 fires were reported in Oklahoma through the middle of April, burning over 115,000 acres (46,575 h). Wildfires even destroyed several buildings in Oklahoma City, Oklahoma. Kansas, Missouri, Nebraska, New Mexico, Arkansas, and Florida all reported higher than normal wildfire activity.

By April 2006, over 22,500 wildfires had been reported across the United States. During the same period of time in 2005, about 9,600 wildfires had been recorded. Some think the 2006 numbers are even higher since firefighters had been so busy they had not reported all the fires.

> **A really large wildfire can create its own wind— sometimes up to 120 miles (193 km) an hour!** ▶

BEING PREPARED

The southern states experience wildfire seasons each year. The wildfire season is usually during the hot summer and windy fall. However, the wildfires of 2005–2006 occurred during the winter months.

People can help prevent wildfires. They can obey **burn bans**. Under a burn ban, campfires and other outdoor fires are not allowed. People can also live in houses built out of materials that do not catch fire easily. They can also make sure that areas around their house do not supply fuel for accidental fires. If a fire does start, people should evacuate their homes and notify the fire department immediately.

This map shows that 124 counties in Texas had burn bans in May 2006.

TEXAS COUNTY BURN BANS IN MAY 2006

■ Counties with Established Burn Bans
□ Counties without Established Burn Bans

STARTING OVER

Thousands of people saw their houses destroyed or damaged in the 2005–2006 wildfires. Many lost all their possessions. The United States government and various charities throughout the country are still helping to find new homes and belongings for the victims of the wildfires. Texas and the other states affected by the wildfires continue to create better ways of preventing and battling future wildfires.

As the Texas wildfires have shown, many firefighters and countless pieces of fire-fighting equipment may not be able to stop a wildfire. A wildfire is one of the most uncontrollable forces on Earth.

GLOSSARY

burn ban (BUHRN BAN) A list of rules to limit outdoor fires in an effort to control wildfires.

chemical reaction (KEH-mih-kuhl ree-AK-shun) A process in which matter is changed into a different form of matter.

drought (DROWT) A long period of dry weather.

evacuate (ih-VA-kyoo-ayt) To leave a place of danger.

extinguish (ik-STIN-gwish) To make something stop burning.

fire retardant (FEYR rih-TAHR-duhnt) A chemical that blocks oxygen from fuel, which slows the growth of fire.

flammable (FLA-muh-buhl) Easily set on fire.

humidity (hyoo-MIH-duh-tee) The amount of moisture in the air.

ignite (ihg-NYT) To start something on fire.

material (muh-TEER-ee-uhl) What something is made of.

temperature (TEHM-pruh-chur) How hot or cold something is.

tornado (tohr-NAY-doh) A spinning column of strong winds that passes over land in a narrow path, often causing much damage.

vegetation (veh-juh-TAY-shun) Plant life.

INDEX

WEB SITES

Due to the changing nature of Internet links, PowerKids Press has developed an online list of Web sites related to the subject of this book. This site is updated regularly. Please use this link to access the list:
http://www.powerkidslinks.com/natnews/texasfire/